PALOMA BLANCA

Illustrated by PAULA KRANZ

WHAT IF I FEEL...

ANGRY

W. Books

Dados Internacionais de Catalogação na Publicação (CIP) de acordo com ISBD

B236w	Barbieri, Paloma Blanca Alves
	What if I feel... angry / Paloma Blanca Alves Barbieri ; traduzido por Karina Barbosa dos Santos ; ilustrado por Paula Kranz. – Jandira : W. Books, 2025.
	32 p. ; 24cm x 24cm. – (What if I feel...)
	Tradução de: E se eu sentir... raiva
	ISBN: 978-65-5294-221-0
	1. Literatura Infantil. 2. Emoções. 3. Sentimentos. 4. Raiva. 5. Psicologia. 6. Saúde. 7. Saúde mental. I. Santos, Karina Barbosa dos. II. Kranz, Paula. III. Título. IV. Série.
	CDD 028.5
2025-1832	CDU 82-93

Elaborada por Vagner Rodolfo da Silva - CRB-8/9410

Índice para catálogo sistemático:
1. Literatura infantil 028.5
2. Literatura infantil 82-93

This book was printed in Melon Slices and Metallophile font.

This is a W. Books publication, a division of Grupo Ciranda Cultural.
© 2025 Ciranda Cultural Editora e Distribuidora Ltda.
Publisher: Elisângela da Silva
Text © Paloma Blanca A. Barbieri
Illustrations © Paula Kranz
Translation: Karina Barbosa dos Santos
Proofreading: Adriane Gozzo
Design: Fernando Nunes / Cover: Natalia Renzzo

First published in June 2025
www.cirandacultural.com.br

"Emotions are the colors of the soul; they are spectacular and incredible. When you don't feel, the world becomes dull and colorless."
William P. Young

I dedicate this book to my gigantic family (especially my mother, Creusa), who has given me and continues to give the most beautiful and diverse emotions!

4

Throughout the day, from the moment I wake up until bedtime, I feel a whirlwind of emotions:

Anger, happiness, sadness, fear...

And I don't always understand them!

Anger is not a fun emotion at all. Whenever it shows up, I turn all red...

... And I don't even realize what I'm saying or doing when this feeling takes over my heart.

Sometimes, I feel angry in the morning, when I have to wake up for school.

But when I hear Mommy calling me with so much love, that feeling goes away.

There are moments when I get angry without even noticing, especially when I start to feel hungry.

RRRRRUUMBLE

10

At those times, Mommy and Daddy notice what's happening and offer me a little snack.

And like magic, the anger and hunger... poof! They disappear in no time!

12

I also get really **angry** when things don't go my way.

Like when I want to play one game, but my friend wants to play another.

When that happens, Mommy always finds a solution and says, "How about playing both games for a little while? That way, everyone will be happy!"

There's something else that makes me really angry...

I even feel like a roaring lion!

ROOOAR

It happens when I have to take a bath on cold days,

or when I'm playing and having so much fun.

17

When someone yells at me or at someone I really like, the anger starts bubbling up inside me.

It feels like I'm going to **explode!**

So I take a deep breath and count to three...
Sometimes, I count until the anger goes away.

1...

2...

3...

NO!

NO!

NOOO!

When Mommy or Daddy says "no" to me,
I cry, scream, and stomp my feet...

... I just don't understand why adults say
that all the time!

23

Some days, I know that **anger** might show up...

... and that's okay!

After all, I can control this feeling and make it disappear...

LIKE THIS!

How do you feel today?

Thankful

Sad

Happy

Angry

Afraid

Loving

Take a little moment to talk about how you're feeling right now.

Talking About Anger

To learn how to handle anger, we first need to understand what caused it. It's important to think about this feeling and talk about it so that we can let it go. Read the questions below and take a moment to reflect on each one.

- What makes you angry? How do you feel or react when that happens?

- What makes you really angry? And what do you do to deal with it?

- What makes you super, super angry? And how do you make that feeling go away?

- When was the last time you felt angry? How did you manage that feeling?

Holding on to negative emotions like anger isn't good for our mind or heart. When we let go of those bad feelings, we feel lighter, happier, and more at peace with ourselves and everything around us. And that's amazing!

Whenever anger shows up, remember that you have options: Take a deep breath, talk about it, or simply wait for it to pass.

Children, Animals, and Feelings

Children are usually fascinated by pets, and it's no wonder why! Besides being loving and great friends, pets bring joy to a home, improve our health, and create a wonderful sense of well-being.

Having a pet (whether it's a kitten, a puppy, or a bunny) can teach children important values like patience, respect, kindness, affection, and responsibility.

Also, when they're with animals, children find the confidence and self-esteem they need to solve their problems and even deal with their own feelings.

A Message for the Family

Discovering emotions can be both surprising and challenging for children, especially when those feelings are difficult to navigate. This book aims to help little ones recognize when and how anger appears and why it's important to experience and express it in a healthy way.

In this journey of emotional discovery, families and educators are invited to see anger from a different perspective: the child's! After all, children have a unique and special way of looking at the world around them.

Managing emotions isn't always easy, whether for adults or children. That's why the earlier kids learn to understand their feelings, the sooner they will develop independence and confidence — essential skills for navigating this incredible journey we all share: life!

PALOMA BLANCA was born in a coastal city in São Paulo. Passionate about languages, she pursued a degree in literature and specialized in translation and teaching.

She has loved writing since childhood; in her stories and poems, she would express everything she felt, as writing became the perfect way for her to explore and understand her emotions. Writing this book has been a true gift, one she hopes to share with families, especially with children who, just like she did in her childhood, wish to learn how to navigate the whirlwind of emotions that arise throughout life.

PAULA KRANZ is the mother of two wonderful girls. When she became a mother, her heart was flooded with countless emotions. She embraced the opportunity to transform all the fear, sadness, anger, and immense joy she experienced into feelings that helped her grow as a person.

Together with her daughters, she reconnected with the magical world of childhood. In recent years, alongside playing pretend, building sandcastles, and doodling, she has also specialized in children's books, illustrating many published works. She is filled with dreams and an eagerness to capture the delicacy and lightness of childhood, bringing to life the magic, the sparkle in children's eyes, and their unique way of seeing the world—something they share with us every single day.